# Love
## is Patient
# Love
## is Kind

# Love
## *is Patient*
# Love
## *is Kind*

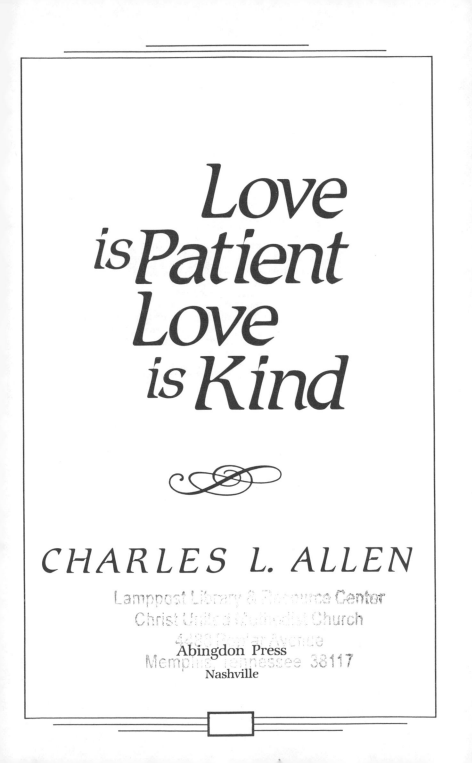

# CHARLES L. ALLEN

Abingdon Press
Nashville

Love Is Patient, Love Is Kind

*Copyright 1989 by Abingdon Press*

This book is printed on acid-free paper.

**Library of Congress Cataloging-in-Publication Data**

Allen, Charles Livingstone, 1913-
  Love is patient, love is kind / Charles L. Allen.
      p.   cm.
  ISBN 0-687-22812-3 (alk. paper)
  1. Bible. N.T. Corinthians, 1st, XIII—Quotations. I. Title
BS2675.5.A54   1989
242'.5—dc19                                            88-37589
                                                            CIP

*Book Design by J.S.Laughbaum*

MANUFACTURED BY THE PARTHENON PRESS AT
NASHVILLE, TENNESSEE, UNITED STATES OF AMERICA

*I dedicate this book
to the mothers of my grandchildren:*

*Kay deMange Allen
Ann Woolsey Allen
Mary Jane Allen Miller*

# Contents

# Acknowledgments

The author gratefully acknowledges the following for permission to reprint material:

Abingdon Press for two excerpts from *Encyclopedia of Wit, Humor, and Wisdom,* edited by Leewin B. Williams. Copyright © 1976 by Chester Williams.

Abingdon Press for an excerpt from *The Seven Words* by Clovis G. Chappell. Copyright © 1952 by Pierce and Smith.

Contemporary Books for the poems "Myself" and "The Kindly Neighbor" from COLLECTED VERSE by Edgar A. Guest. Copyright © 1934 by Contemporary Books, Inc.

The Markham Archives for "Outwitted," by Edwin Markham.

*Love*
*is Patient*
*Love*
*is Kind*

# *Introduction*

## THROUGH A CRYSTAL PRISM

Paul, in three verses, very short, gives us an amazing analysis of what love is. It is a compound thing, he tells us. It is like light. As you have seen a man of science take a beam of light and pass it through a crystal prism, as you have seen it come out on the other side of the prism broken up into its component colors—red and blue and yellow and violet and orange and all the colors of the rainbow—so Paul passes Love through the magnificent prism of his inspired intellect, and it comes out on the other side broken up into its elements.

The Spectrum of Love has nine ingredients:

Patience: "Love suffereth long."
Kindness: "And is kind."
Generosity: "Love envieth not."
Humility: "Love vaunteth not itself, it is not puffed up."
Courtesy: "Doth not behave itself unseemly."
Unselfishness: "Seeketh not her own."
Good Temper: "Is not easily provoked."

Guilelessness: "Thinketh no evil."
Sincerity: "Rejoiceth not in iniquity, but rejoiceth in the
truth."

—Henry Drummond
*The Greatest Thing in the World*

Paul points out that in love there are nine
life-coloring attitudes. These are the nine colors of
love: Patience—kindness—generosity—humility—
courtesy—unselfishness—good temper—guilelessness
—sincerity.

I have collected the quotations in this book over the
years of my ministry.

I express appreciation to Marisa Alanis for her help
with the manuscript.

—Charles L. Allen

# Patience

### . . . "Love Suffereth Long"

---

Suffering—Patience—Leniency
Pain and Distress—Loss—Tolerance

---

א

## Suffering

When drooping pleasure turns to grief,
  And trembling faith is changed to fear,
The murmuring wind, the quivering leaf,
  Shall softly tell us, Thou art near!

Oliver Wendell Holmes, "Hymn of Trust"

In suffering, we learn to pray best of all.

Harold A. Bosley, On Final Ground

We need to suffer so that we may learn to pity.

Letitia E. Landon

## Patience

Never a tear bedims the eye
That time and patience will not dry.

Bret Harte, "The Lost Galleon"

Patience is bitter, but its fruit is sweet.

Jean Jacques Rousseau, *Émile*

ℵ

Patience is a bitter plant, but it bears sweet fruit.

German Proverb

ℵ

We count them happy which endure. Ye have heard of the patience of Job. (James 5:11)

ℵ

*Lines Written in Her Breviary*

Let nothing disturb thee,
Nothing affright thee;
All things are passing,
God never changeth;
Patient endurance
Attaineth to all things;
Who God possesseth
In nothing is wanting;
Along God sufficeth.

Saint Teresa (1515-1582), translated by Henry W. Longfellow

*Peace, Perfect Peace*

Peace, perfect peace,
by thronging duties pressed?
To do the will of Jesus: this is rest.

Peace, perfect peace,
with sorrows surging round?
On Jesus' bosom naught but calm is
  found.

Peace, perfect peace,
with loved ones far away?
In Jesus' keeping we are safe,
  and they.

Edward H. Bickersteth

ℵ

Still achieving, still pursuing,
Learn to labour and to wait.

Henry W. Longfellow, "A Psalm of Life"

ℵ

## Leniency

Let all bitterness, and wrath, and anger, and clamour, and evil speaking, be put away from you, with all malice. (Ephesians 4:31).

And be ye kind one to another, tenderhearted, forgiving one another, even as God for Christ's sake hath forgiven you. (Ephesians 4:32)

☙

If we could read the secret history of our enemies, we should find in each man's life sorrow and suffering enough to disarm all hostility.

Henry W. Longfellow, "Driftwood"

☙

## Pain and Distress

The pain of the mind is worse than the pain of the body.

Publilius Syrus, *Sententiae*

☙

There was never yet philosopher
That could endure the toothache patiently,
However they have writ the style of gods
And made a push at chance and sufferance.

William Shakespeare, *Much Ado About Nothing*

We look before and after,
    And pine for what is not
Our sincerest laughter
    With some pain is fraught;
Our sweetest songs are those that tell of saddest
        thought.

Yet if we could scorn
    Hate and pride and fear,
If we were things born
    Not to shed a tear,
I know not how thy joy we ever should come near.

Percy B. Shelley, "To the Skylark"

Nothing begins, and nothing ends,
    That is not paid with moan;
For we are born in others' pain,
    And perish in our own.

Francis Thompson, "Daisy"

## Loss

Wise men ne'er sit and wail their loss,
But cheerily seek how to redress their harms.

William Shakespeare, *Henry VI, Part III*

'Tis better to have loved and lost
Than never to have loved at all.

Alfred, Lord Tennyson, "In Memoriam"

## Tolerance

Tolerance implies a respect for another person, not
because the person is wrong, or even right, but because
that person is human.

John Cogley, "A Word for Tolerance"

## *Intolerance*

And when religious sects ran mad,
    He held, in spite of all learning,
That if a man's belief is bad,
    It will not be improved by burning.

W. M. Praed

We are only miserable so far as we think ourselves so.

Sannazaro, *Ecloga Octava*

Misery makes sport to mock itself.

William Shakespeare, *Richard II*

# Kindness

## . . . *"And Is Kind"*

---

### Kindness—Compassion—Mercy
### Sympathy

---

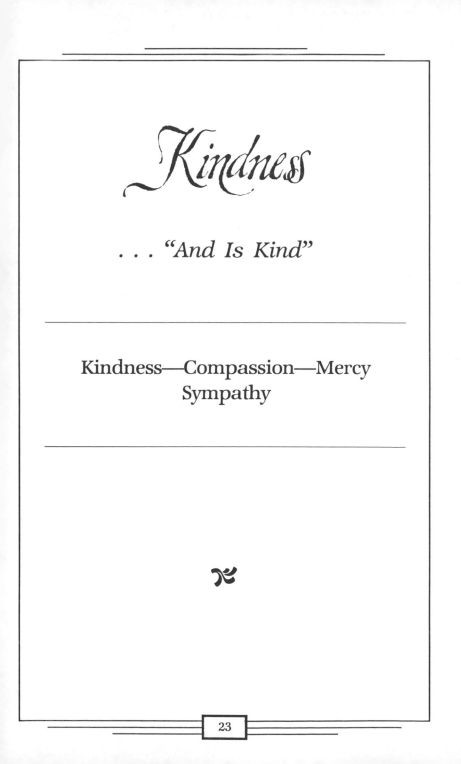

## Kindness

That best portion of a good
　　man's life,
His little, nameless, unremembered acts
Of kindness and of love.

William Wordsworth, "Tintern Abbey"

א

### *Jesus, United by Thy Grace*

Jesus, united by thy grace,
And each to each endeared,
With confidence we seek thy face,
And know our prayer is heard.

Touched by the lodestone of thy love,
Let us in all things grow,
Till thou hast made us free indeed
And spotless here below.

This is the bond of perfectness,
Thy spotless charity;
O let us, still we pray, possess
The mind that was in thee.

Charles Wesley

## Take Time to Be Holy

Take time to be holy,
Speak oft with thy Lord;
Abide in him always,
And feed on his Word;
Make friends of God's children,
Help those who are weak,
Forgetting in nothing
His blessing to seek.

William D. Longstaff

## There's a Wideness in God's Mercy

There's a wideness in God's mercy,
Like the wideness of the sea;
There's a kindness in his justice,
Which is more than liberty.
There is welcome for the sinner,
And more graces for the good;
There is mercy with the Savior;
There is healing in his blood.

For the love of Good is broader
Than the measure of man's mind;
And the heart of the Eternal
Is most wonderfully kind.
If our love were but more simple,
We should take him at his word;
And our lives would be all sunshine
In the sweetness of our Lord.

Frederick W. Faber

*from "The Kindly Neighbor"*

I have a kindly neighbor, one who stands
Beside my gate and chats with me awhile,
Gives me the glory of his radiant smile
And comes at times to help with willing hands.

No station high or rank this man commands;
He, too, must trudge, as I, the long day's mile,
And yet, devoid of pomp or gaudy style,
He has a worth exceeding stocks or lands.

To him I go when sorrow's at my door;
On him I lean when burdens come my way;
Together oft we talk our trials o'er,
And there is warmth in each good-night we say.

A kindly neighbor! Wars and strife shall end
When man has made the man next door his friend.

Edgar A. Guest

## Compassion

### *Thou Hidden Source of Calm Repose*

Thou hidden source of calm repose,
Thou all-sufficient love divine,
My help and refuge from my foes,
Secure I am if thou art mine;
And lo! from sin and grief and shame,
I hide me, Jesus, in thy name.

Thy mighty name salvation is,
And keeps my happy soul above;
Comfort it brings, and power and peace,
And joy and everlasting love:
To me, with thy great name, are given
Pardon and holiness and heaven.

Charles Wesley

א

## Mercy

We hand folks over to God's mercy, and show none
ourselves.

George Eliot, *Adam Bede*

He hath showed thee, O man, what is good; and what doth the Lord require of thee, but to do justly, and to love mercy, and to walk humbly with thy God? (Micah 6:8)

For he shall have judgment without mercy, that hath shewed no mercy; and mercy rejoiceth against judgment. (James 2:13)

Blessed are the merciful: for they shall obtain mercy. (Matthew 5:7)

## The Divine Image

To Mercy, Pity, Peace, and Love
All pray in their distress;
And to these virtues of delight
Return their thankfulness.

For Mercy, Pity, Peace, and Love
Is God, our Father dear,
And Mercy, Pity, Peace, and Love
Is man, His child and care.

For Mercy has a human heart,
Pity a human face,
And Love, the human form divine,
And Peace, the human dress.

Then every man, of every clime,
That prays in his distress,
Prays to the human form divine,
Love, Mercy, Pity, Peace.

And all must love the human form,
In heathen, Turk, or Jew;
Where Mercy, Love, and Pity dwell
There God is dwelling too.

William Blake

### The Cross

Talk not of Justice and her scales of woe,
We know no justice, weighing gain and loss,
Save the balancing arms of love held wide
That cannot sway or falter to and fro,
Mercy on this side and the other side,
The adamantine justice of the Cross.

Eva Gore-Booth

א

The quality of mercy is not strain'd,
It droppeth as the gentle rain from heaven
Upon the place beneath. It is twice bless'd:
It blesseth him that gives and him that takes.
'Tis mightiest in the mightiest: it becomes
The throned monarch better than his crown:
His sceptre shows the force of temporal power,
The attribute to awe and majesty,
Wherein doth sit the dread and fear of kings;
But mercy is above this sceptred sway,
It is enthroned in the hearts of kings
It is an attribute to God himself;
And earthly power doth then show likest God's,
When mercy seasons justice.

William Shakespeare, *The Merchant of Venice*

## Sympathy

Rejoice with them that do rejoice, and weep with them that weep. (Romans 12:15)

❧

Open thy gate of mercy, gracious God!
My soul flies through these wounds to seek out Thee.

William Shakespeare, *Henry VI, Part III*

❧

*Blest Be the Tie That Binds*

Blest be the tie that binds
Our hearts in Christian love:
The fellowship of kindred minds
Is like to that above.

We share each other's woes,
Our mutual burdens bear,
And often for each other flows
The sympathizing tear.

John Fawcett

ℵ

### *Be Still, My Soul, the Lord Is on Thy Side*

Be still, my soul: the Lord is on thy side!
Bear patiently the cross of grief or pain;
Leave to thy God to order and provide
In ev'ry change He faithful will remain.
Be still, my soul: thy best, thy heav'nly friend
Thru thorny ways leads to a joyful end.

Be still, my soul: thy God doth undertake
To guide thy future as he has the past;
Thy hope, thy confidence let nothing shake
All now mysterious shall be bright at last.
Be still, my soul: the waves and winds still know
His voice who ruled them while he dwelt below.

Be still, my soul: the hour is hast'ning on
To guide the future as he has the past;
When disappointment, grief, and fear are gone,
Sorrow forgot, love's purest joys restored.
Be still, my soul: when change and tears are past,
All safe and blessed we shall meet at last.

Katharina von Schlegel, translated by Jane L. Borthwick

# Generosity

### . . . *"Love Envieth Not"*

---

Envy—Magnanimity
Charity

---

# Envy

There is a time in every man's education when he arrives at the conviction that envy is ignorance; that limitation is suicide; that he must take himself for better, for worse, as his portion; that though the wide universe is full of good, no kernel of nourishing corn can come to him but through his toil bestowed on that plot of ground which is given him to till. The power which resides in him is new in Nature, and none but he knows what that is which he can do, nor does he know until he has tried.

Ralph W. Emerson, "Self-Reliance"

א

Thou shalt not covet thy neighbor's house, thou shalt not covet thy neighbor's wife, nor his manservant, nor his maidservant, nor his ox, nor his ass, nor any thing that is thy neighbor's. (Exodus 20:17)

א

The truest sign of being born with great qualities is to be born without envy.

La Rochefoucauld, *Maxims*

# Magnanimity

Life is short, and we have never too much time for gladdening the hearts of those who are traveling the dark journey with us. Oh, be swift to love, make haste to be kind!

Henri F. Amiel, *Journal*

Then said Jesus, Father, forgive them; for they know not what they do. (Luke 23:34)

### Blest Are the Pure in Heart

Blest are the pure in heart,
For they shall see our God;
The secret of the Lord is theirs,
Their soul is Christ's abode.

Still to the lowly soul
He doth himself impart,
And for his dwelling and his throne
Selects the pure in heart.

Lord, we thy presence seek;
May ours this blessing be:
O give the pure and lowly heart,
A temple meet for thee.

John Keble

## Charity

And as ye would that men should do to you, do ye also to them likewise. (Luke 6:31)

To do him any wrong was to beget
A kindness from him, for his heart was rich,
Of such fine mold that if you sowed therein
The seed of Hate, it blossomed Charity.

Alfred, Lord Tennyson, "Queen Mary"

In charity there is no excess.

Francis Bacon, *Essays*

א

With malice toward none;
With charity for all;
With firmness in the right, as God gives us to see the
    right,
Let us strive on to finish the work we are in;
To bind up the nation's wounds;
To care for him who shall have borne the battle,
And for his widow,
And his orphan—
To do all which may achieve and cherish a just and
    lasting peace among ourselves,
And with all nations.

Abraham Lincoln, from the Second Inaugural Address,
March 4, 1865

# Humility

## . . . "Love Vaunteth Not Itself, Is Not Puffed Up"

## Humility—Meekness

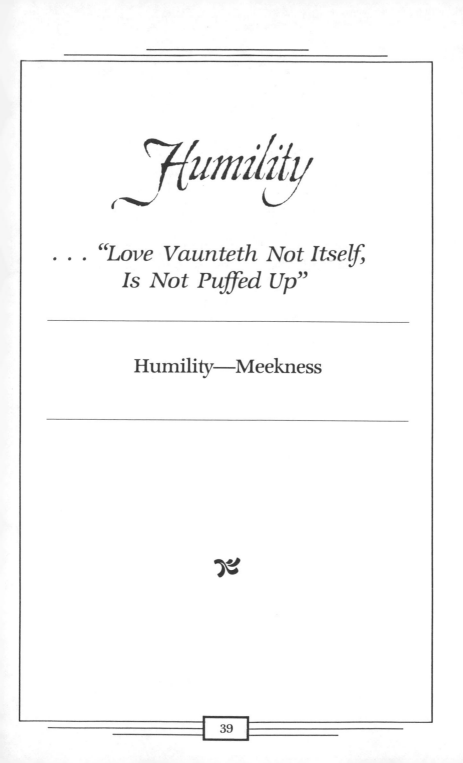

# Humility

I would not ask Thee that my days
   Should flow quite smoothly on and on,
Lest I should learn to love the world
   Too well, ere all my time was done.

I would not ask Thee that my work
   Should never bring me pain nor fear;
Lest I should learn to work alone,
   And never wish thy presence near.

I would not ask Thee that my friends
   Should always kind and constant be;
Lest I should learn to lay my faith
   In them alone, and not in thee.

But I would ask a humble heart,
   A changeless will to work and wake,
A firm faith in Thy providence,
   The rest—'tis thine to give or take.

Alfred Norris

Humble we must be if to heaven we go;
High is the roof there; but the gate is low.

Robert Herrick

Humility, that low, sweet root,
From which all heavenly virtues shoot.

Thomas Moore, *Loves of the Angels*

I pray not that
Men tremble at
My power of place,
    And lordly sway;
I only pray for simple grace
To look my neighbor in the face
    Full honestly from day to day.

James Whitcomb Riley

Patient, resigned and humble wills
Impregnable resist all ills.

Thomas Ken

Be not too ready to condemn
   The wrong thy brothers may have done:
Ere ye too harshly censure them
   For human faults, ask, "Have I none?"

Eliza Cook

ૐ

The true way to be humble is not to stoop until you are smaller than yourself, but to stand at your real height against some higher nature that will show you what the real smallness of your greatest greatness is.

Phillips Brooks

ૐ

Pride changes angels into devils. Humility changes people into angels.

Augustine of Hippo

ૐ

Too much humility is pride.

German Proverb

He that is down needs fear no fall,
  He that is low, no pride;
He that is humble ever shall
  Have God to be his guide.

I am content with what I have,
  Little be it or much:
And, Lord, contentment still I crave,
  Because Thou savest such.

Fullness to such a burden is
  That go on pilgrimage:
Here little, and hereafter bliss,
  Is best from age to age.

John Bunyan, *The Pilgrim's Progress*

O wad some Power the giftie gie us
To see oursels as ithers see us!
It wad frae monie a blunder free us,
  An' foolish notion.
What airs in dress an' gait wad lea'e us,
An' ev'n devotion!

Robert Burns, from "To a Louse"

### *from "God's Two Dwellings"*

Though Heaven be high, the gate is low,
And he that comes in there must bow:
   The lofty Looks shall ne'er
    Have entrance there.

O God! since Thou delight'st to rest
In the humble contrite breast,
   First make me so to be,
    Then dwell with me.

Thomas Washbourne

I believe the first test of a truly great man is his humility.

John Ruskin

Be not wise in thine own eyes: fear the Lord, and depart from evil. (Proverbs 3:7)

He that goeth about as a talebearer revealeth secrets: therefore meddle not with him that flattereth with his lips. (Proverbs 20:19)

Life is a long lesson in humility.

James M. Barrie

Humility is to make a right estimate of oneself.

Charles Spurgeon, *Gleanings: Humility*

## Meekness

Take my yoke upon you, and learn of me; for I am meek and lowly in heart: and ye shall find rest unto your souls. (Matthew 11:29)

But the meek shall inherit the earth; and shall delight themselves in the abundance of peace. (Psalm 37:11)

I was too ambitious in my deed,
And thought to distance all men in success,
Till God came on me, marked the place, and said,
"Ill-doer, henceforth keep within this line,
Attempting less than others"—and I stand
And work among Christ's little ones, content.

Elizabeth Barrett Browning

# *Courtesy*

## *Courtesy . . . "Doth Not Behave Itself Unseemly"*

Courtesy—Behavior—Politeness
Respect/Self-respect—Manners

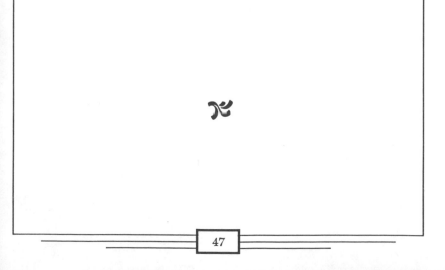

## Courtesy

Life is short, but there is always time for courtesy.

Ralph W. Emerson, *Uncollected Lectures*: "Social Aims"

🕉

It is almost a definition of a gentleman to say that he is one who never inflicts pain.

John Henry Newman, "The Idea of a University"

🕉

To meet men and women with laughter
    on my lips and love in my heart;
To be gentle, kind, and courteous through all the hours
To approach the night with weariness that ever woos sleep,
    and the joy that comes from work well done—
This is how I desire to waste wisely my days.

Thomas Dekker

🕉

## Behavior

Behavior is a mirror that shows us our images.

Johann Wolfgang von Goethe, *Elective Affinities*

Therefore all things whatsoever ye would that men should do to you, do ye even so to them: for this is the law and the prophets. (Matthew 7:12)

## Politeness

One of the greatest victories you can gain over people is to beat them at politeness.

Josh Billings (Henry Wheeler Shaw)

Politeness smoothes wrinkles.

Joubert, Pensées

## Respect/Self-respect

This above all: to thine own self be true;
And it must follow, as the night the day,
Thou canst not then be false to any man.

William Shakespeare, Hamlet

Never esteem anything as an advantage to you that makes you break your word or lose your self-respect.

Marcus Aurelius, *Meditations*

Be ye angry, and sin not: let not the sun go down upon your wrath. (Ephesians 4:26)

Self-reverence, self-knowledge, self-control,
These three alone lead life to sovereign power.

Alfred, Lord Tennyson, "Oenone"

You shall love your neighbor as yourself. (Galatians 5:14 RSV)

## Myself

I have to live with myself, and so
I want to be fit for myself to know,
I want to be able, as days go by,
Always to look myself straight in the eye;
I don't want to stand, with the setting sun,
And hate myself for the things I've done.

I don't want to keep on a closet shelf,
A lot of secrets about myself,
And fool myself, as I come and go,
Into thinking that nobody else will know
The kind of a man that I really am;
I don't want to dress up myself in sham.

I want to go out with my head erect,
I want to deserve all men's respect;
But here in the struggle for fame and pelf,
I want to be able to like myself.
I don't want to look at myself and know
That I'm bluster and bluff and empty show.

I never can hide myself from me;
I see what others may never see;
I know what others may never know;
I never can fool myself, and so,
Whatever happens, I want to be
Self-respecting and conscience free.

Edgar A. Guest

None but one can harm you,
None but yourself who are your greatest foe;
He that respects himself is safe from others;
He wears a coat of mail that none can pierce.

Henry W. Longfellow, "The Foe Within"

The reverence of a man's self is, next to religion, the chiefest bridle of all vices.

Francis Bacon, *New Atlantis*

## Manners

I can make a lord, but only God Almighty can make a gentleman.

James I of England

Manners are the happy ways of doing things; each one a stroke of genius or of love, now repeated and hardened into usage.

Ralph W. Emerson, *Conduct of Life*

꒒

A debutante went to visit her grandmother. The old woman was distressed by her granddaughter's use of slang. Not wishing to appear stern and demanding, she decided nevertheless that she would reprimand her granddaughter.

One evening as they were sitting together the grandmother said gently, "Dear, there are just two words I want you to refrain from using. One is 'swell' and the other is 'lousy.'"

"All right," replied the granddaughter agreeably, "what are they?"

Leewin B. Williams, *Encyclopedia of Wit, Humor, and Wisdom*

꒒

Most arts require long study and application; but the most useful of all, that of pleasing, only the desire.

Lord Chesterfield, *Letters*

# Unselfishness

## . . . *"Seeketh Not Her Own"*

---

Selfishness/Unselfishness—Generosity
Liberality—Selflessness

---

א

## Selfishness/Unselfishness

Selfishness is the greatest curse of the human race.

William E. Gladstone

ℵ

Lord, help me live from day to day
In such a self-forgetful way
That even when I kneel to pray
My prayers will be for OTHERS.

Charles D. Meigs, "Others"

ℵ

### Lead, Kindly Light

Lead, kindly Light, amid th'encircling
gloom,
Lead thou me on!
The night is dark, and I am far from
home;
Lead thou me on!
Keep thou my feet; I do not ask to see
The distant scene; one step enough for
me.

John Henry Newman

## Generosity

It is more blessed to give than to receive. (Acts 20:35)

ℵ

Then Peter said, Silver and gold have I none; but such as I have give I thee: In the name of Jesus Christ of Nazareth rise up and walk. (Acts 3:6)

ℵ

We make a living by what we get, but we make a life by what we give.

Winston S. Churchill

ℵ

Every man according as he purposeth in his heart, so let him give; not grudgingly, or of necessity: for God loveth a cheerful giver. (II Corinthians 9:7)

What can I give Him
Poor as I am?
If I were a shepherd,
I would give Him a lamb,
If I were a Wise Man,
I would do my part,—
But what I can I give Him,
Give my heart.

Christina G. Rossetti, "A Christmas Carol"

Liberality consists less in giving much than in giving at the right time.

Jean de la Bruyère, *Les Caractères*

Generosity gives help rather than advice.

Luc de Clapiers Vauvenargues

## Liberality

Frugality is good, if liberality be joined with it. The first is leaving off superfluous expenses; the last bestowing them to the benefit of others that need. The first without the last begets covetousness; the last without the first begets prodigality. Both together make an excellent temper. Happy the place where that is found.

William Penn, *Fruits of Solitude*

א

Some witty person once said: "There are three kinds of givers—the flint, the sponge, and the honeycomb." To get anything out of the flint you must hammer it, and then you get only chips and sparks. To get water out of a sponge you must squeeze it, and the more you squeeze the more you will get. But the honeycomb just overflows with its own sweetness. Some people are stingy and hard; they give nothing away if they can help it. Others are good-natured; they yield to pressure, and the more they are pressed the more they will give. A few delight in giving, without being asked at all; and of these the Bible says: "The Lord loveth a cheerful giver."

Leewin B. Williams, *Encyclopedia of Wit, Humor, and Wisdom*

## Selflessness

### *Outwitted*

He drew a circle that shut me out—
Heretic, rebel, a thing to flout.
But Love and I had the wit to win:
We drew a circle that took him in!

Edwin Markham

### *St. Francis' Prayer*

Lord, make me an instrument of Thy peace.
Where there is hate, may I bring love;
Where offense, may I bring pardon;
May I bring union in place of discord;
Truth, replacing error;
Faith, where once there was doubt;
Hope, for despair;
Light, where was darkness;
Joy to replace sadness.
Make me not to so crave to be loved as to love.
Help me to learn that in giving I may receive;
In forgetting self, I may find life eternal.

St. Francis of Assisi (1182-1226)

*My Kingdom*

I do not ask for any crown
    But that which all may win;
Nor try to conquer any world
    Except the one within.
Be Thou my guide until I find
    Led by a tender hand,
The happy kingdom in myself
    And dare to take command.

Louisa May Alcott

# Good Temper

## . . . *"Is Not Easily Provoked"*

Temper—Anger
Self-control—Disposition

# Temper

## *The Passionate Sword*

Temper my spirit, O Lord,
  Burn out its alloy,
And make it a pliant steel for Thy wielding,
  Not a clumsy toy;
A blunt, iron thing in my hands
  That blunder and destroy.

Temper my spirit, O Lord,
  Keep it long in the fire;
Make it one with the flame. Let it share
  That up-reaching desire.
Grasp it, Thyself, O my God;
  Swing it straighter and higher!

Jean Starr Untermeyer

**א**

Cast thy burden upon the Lord, and he shall sustain thee: he shall never suffer the righteous to be moved. (Psalm 55:22)

**א**

A tart temper never mellows with age, and a sharp tongue is the only edged tool that grows keener with constant use.

Washington Irving, "Rip Van Winkle"

Our happiness and unhappiness depend as much on our turn of mind as on fortune.

La Rochefoucauld, Maxims

## Anger

Reckon the days in which you have not been angry. "I used to be angry every day; now every other day; then every third and fourth day." And if you miss it so long as thirty days, offer a sacrifice of thanksgiving to God.

Epictetus, Discourses

Be not hasty in thy spirit to be angry: for anger resteth in the bosom of fools. (Ecclesiastes 7:9)

All anger is not sinful, because some degree of it is inevitable. It becomes sinful and contradicts the rule of Scripture when it is founded on slight and inadequate provocation and when it continues long.

William Paley

The greatest remedy for anger is delay.

Seneca, *De Ira*

A soft answer turneth away wrath: but grievous words stir up anger. (Proverbs 15:1)

Anybody can become angry. But to be angry with the right person to the right degree, at the right time, for the right purpose, and in the right way is not within everybody's power.

Aristotle, *Nicomachean Ethics*

Anger is never without an argument, but seldom with a good one.

Lord Halifax, *Works*

To be angry is to revenge the faults of others upon ourselves.

Alexander Pope, *Thoughts on Various Subjects*

א

We boil at different degrees.

Ralph W. Emerson, "Eloquence"

א

But I say unto you, That whosoever is angry with his brother without a cause shall be in danger of the judgment: and whosoever shall say to his brother, Raca, shall be in danger of the council: but whosoever shall say, Thou fool, shall be in danger of hell fire. (Matthew 5:22)

א

Whenever you are angry, be assured, that it is not only a present evil, but that you have increased a habit.

Epictetus, *Discourses*

## Self-control

In taking revenge, a man is but even with his enemy; but in passing it over, he is superior.

Francis Bacon, "Of Revenge"

What government is the best? The one that teaches us to govern ourselves.

Johann Wolfgang von Goethe, *Sprüche in Prosa*

## Disposition

No one is free who cannot command oneself.

Pythagoras

He that is slow to anger is better than the mighty; and he that ruleth his spirit than he that taketh a city. (Proverbs 16:32)

# Guilelessness

## . . . *"Thinketh No Evil"*

---

## Suspicion—Trust/Distrust

---

## Suspicion

### It Never Comes Again

There are gains for all our losses,
   There are balms for all our pain,
But when youth, the dream, departs,
It takes something from our hearts,
   And it never comes again.

We are stronger, and are better,
   Under manhood's sterner reign;
Still we feel that something sweet
Followed youth, with flying feet,
   And will never come again.

Something beautiful is vanished,
   And we sigh for it in vain;
We behold it everywhere,
On the earth, and in the air,
   But it never comes again.

Richard Henry Stoddard

א

Suspicion is no less an enemy to virtue than to happiness. He that is already corrupt is naturally suspicious, and he that becomes suspicious will quickly be corrupt.

Samuel Johnson, *The Rambler*

## Trust/Distrust

Thou shalt love thy neighbor as thyself. (Leviticus 19:18)

א

I read of a great artist who was spending a few days in a humble home. It so happened that while he was a guest the little girl of the family had a birthday. Among the presents she received was a silk fan. It was a fairly ordinary affair, but when she showed it to the artist he said, "If you will let me keep this for a little while, I will paint you a picture on it."

But she snatched it away, saying, "You shan't spoil my fan."

If she had only trusted him, he would have given it back with its beauty and worth increased a thousand-fold.

Clovis G. Chappell, *The Seven Words*

א

Better trust all and be deceived,
    And weep that trust and that deceiving,
Than doubt one heart, that if believed
    Had blessed one's life with true believing.
Oh, in this mocking world too fast
    The doubting fiend o'ertakes our youth;
Better be cheated to the last
    Than lose the blessed hope of truth.

Frances Anne Kemble

Trust men and they will be true to you; treat them greatly, and they will show themselves great.

Ralph W. Emerson, *Essays*

What loneliness is more lonely than distrust?

George Eliot, *Middlemarch*

# Sincerity

## . . . "Rejoiceth Not in Iniquity, but Rejoiceth in the Truth"

Sincerity—Hyprocrisy
Deceit—Truth

ℵ

# Sincerity

Sincerity is impossible, unless it pervades the whole being and the pretence of it saps the very foundation of character.

James Russell Lowell, *Essays*: "Pope"

꒳

The sincere alone can recognise sincerity.

Thomas Carlyle, *Heroes and Hero Worship*

꒳

## *Prayer*

I often say my prayers,
But do I ever pray;
And do the wishes of my heart
Go with the words I say?

I may as well kneel down
And worship gods of stone,
As offer to the living God
A prayer of words alone.

For words without the heart
The Lord will never hear:
Nor will he to those lips attend
Whose prayers are not sincere.

John Burton

## Hypocrisy

Hypocrisy is the homage that vice pays to virtue.

La Rochefoucauld, *Maxims*

Woe unto you, scribes and Pharisees, hypocrites! for ye are like unto whited sepulchres, which indeed appear beautiful outward, but are within full of dead men's bones, and of all uncleanness. (Matthew 23:27)

*As We Pray*

Only, O Lord, in Thy dear love
Fit us for perfect rest above;
And help us this and every day,
To live more nearly as we pray.

John Keble

## Two Went Up to the Temple to Pray

Two went to pray? Oh, rather say
One went to brag, the other to pray;
One stands up close and treads on high
Where the other dares not send his eye;
One nearer to God's altar trod,
The other to the altar's God.

Richard Crashaw

## O For a Heart to Praise My God

O for a heart to praise my God,
A heart from sin set free,
A heart that always feels thy blood
So freely shed for me;

A heart in every thought renewed
And full of love divine,
Perfect and right and pure and good,
A copy, Lord, of thine.

Thy nature, gracious Lord, impart;
Come quickly from above;
Write thy new name upon my heart,
Thy new, best name of Love.

Charles Wesley

## Deceit

O, what a tangled web we weave,
When first we practise to deceive!

Walter Scott, "Marmion"

א

## Truth

The highest compact we can make with our fellow
is—Let there be truth between us two forevermore.

Ralph W. Emerson, *Conduct of Life*

א

In the mountains of truth, you never climb in vain.

Friedrich Nietzsche, *Thus Spake Zarathustra*

א

The truth is always the strongest argument.

Sophocles, *Phaedra*

Time is precious, but truth is more precious than time.

Benjamin Disraeli, speech given at Aylesbury, Sept. 11, 1865

א־

It is one thing to wish to have truth on our side, and another to wish sincerely to be on the side of truth.

Richard Whately, "On the Love of Truth"

א־

## O Christ, the Way

O Christ, the Way, the Truth, the Life,
Show me the living way,
That in the tumult and the strife
I may not go astray.

Teach me Thy Truth, O Christ, my Light,
The Truth that makes me free,
That in the darkness and the night
My trust shall be in Thee.

The Life that Thou alone canst give,
Impart in love to me,
That I may in Thy presence live,
And ever be like Thee.

George L. Squier

### The Bible

We search the world for truth. We cull
The good, the true, the beautiful,
From graven stone and written scroll,
And all old flower-fields of the soul;
And, weary seekers of the best,
We come back laden from our quest,
To find that all the sages said
Is in the Book our mothers read.

John G. Whittier

### Be True

Thou must be true thyself
   If thou the truth wouldst teach;
Thy soul must overflow if thou
   Another's soul wouldst reach!
It needs the overflow of heart
   To give the lips full speech.

Think truly, and thy thoughts
   Shall the world's famine feed;
Speak truly, and each word of thine
   Shall be a fruitful seed;
Live truly, and thy life shall be
   A great and noble creed.

Horatius Bonar

Though love repine, and reason chafe,
There came a voice without reply,—
"'Tis man's perdition to be safe,
When for the truth he ought to die."

Ralph W. Emerson, "Sacrifice"

Truth, crushed to earth shall rise
    again,—
The eternal years of God are hers;
But Error, wounded, writhes in pain,
And dies among his worshippers.

William Cullen Bryant, "The Battle-Field"